I Dream for You a World:
A Covenant for Our Children

Charisse Carney-

12/2009

Presented by **THE JAMESTOWN PROJECT**   Foreword by **TAVIS SMILEY**

By Charisse Carney-Nunes   Illustrated by Ann Marie Williams

This book is dedicated to the spirit of our ancestors and the radiance of the children. If there is to be a "Covenant Movement" then it is on our ancestors' shoulders that we must stand, and it is the radiance of our children's hearts and minds that lights our way.

The author thanks the Jamestown Project for making this book a reality. The Jamestown Project is a nonprofit, nonpartisan think/action tank dedicated to making real the promise of American democracy. An organization made up of primarily women and people of color, Jamestown knows that a healthy, democratic society that is truly inclusive of all voices requires thoughtful and informed citizens, and that we must start by educating those with the most optimism and promise for tomorrow—our children.

Published by Brand Nu Words, LLC

To order additional copies of this book contact:
Brand Nu Words
1314 Fairmont St. NW
Washington, DC 20009
www.BrandNuWords.com
Email: info@JamestownProject.org
877-387-1314

Written by Charisse Carney-Nunes
Illustrated by Ann Marie Williams

In collaboration with The Jamestown Project

Text and Artwork Copyright © by The Smiley Group

ISBN: 978-0-9748142-3-0

Library of Congress Control Number: 2006909990

First Edition: February 2007

Printed in China

A Note from Tavis Smiley

"So today, my child, please work with me
For just as surely as I dream
We can build up our tomorrow
We'll create a Freedom Team"

— I DREAM FOR YOU A WORLD

In creating a "Freedom Team" it is imperative that we are ever mindful of who will ultimately hold the torch of progress—our children. Every year my dedication to the principles set forth in the COVENANT WITH BLACK AMERICA is reinforced not only by the commencement of the State of the Black Union, but by the initiatives that actually sprout from the robust discussion of these COVENANT agenda items. I DREAM FOR YOU A WORLD is one of those efforts.

I DREAM FOR YOU A WORLD is a covenant that we are making with our children, the future leaders of the "Freedom Team" who will propel forward to create the world we presently dream for them. It is to be shared with the young and the old. It is to be used as a call and response tool that will encourage verbal affirmation of their potential to dream, to create and to just "be."

I am proud that this project had its roots in the COVENANT, and that the Jamestown Project has moved the COVENANT principles into action to empower our youth. My hope is that the poetic pages of this book will be internalized by someone you love who will define their place in the world as we know it today, and who will one day play an active role in designing that world that we dream of for tomorrow.

If the COVENANT is going to have long-term meaning, we cannot omit our children from the bigger picture of changing the landscape for their future. Share this book with them. Let it serve as an early introduction to the principles that their elders identify as COVENANT principles. Let it be the first step that we encourage our children to take toward accountability for designing their dreams and building a better tomorrow.

Yours in moving forward,
Tavis Smiley

I dream for you a world

Where you'll grow healthy and grow strong

Where you'll be well and won't be sick

And where we'll thrive all our days long

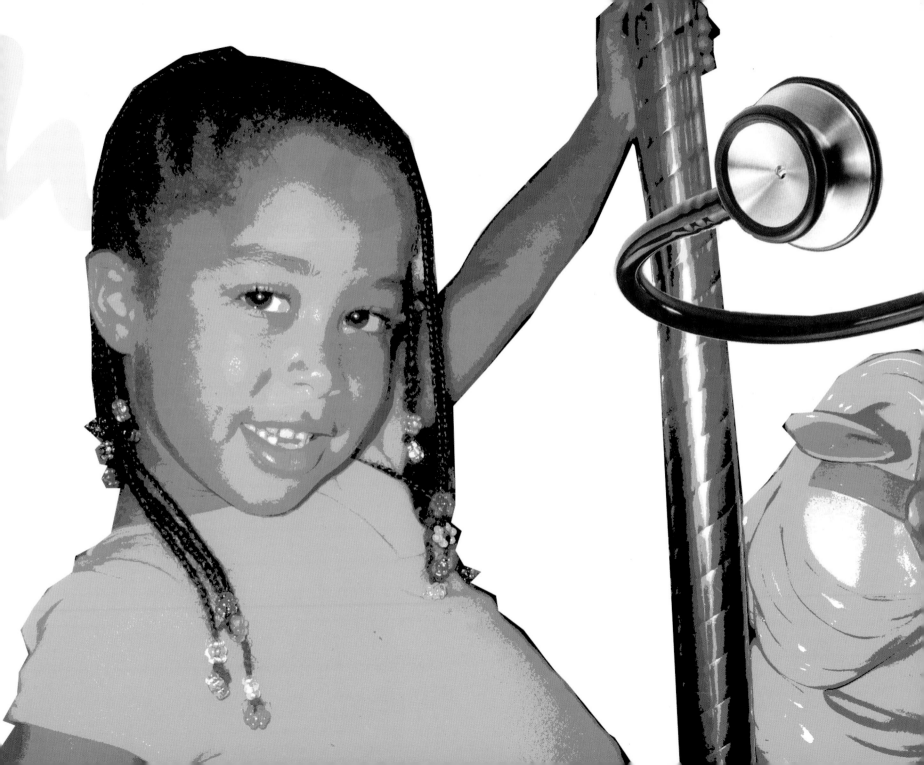

Dream. Wish. Hope. Soar.

Education

I dream for you a world

Where education frees your mind
To dream and think and feel and hope
Where you will never fall behind

I AM A STAR!

I dream for you a world

That is just and fair and free

Where your brothers aren't confined

And where we'll build up liberty

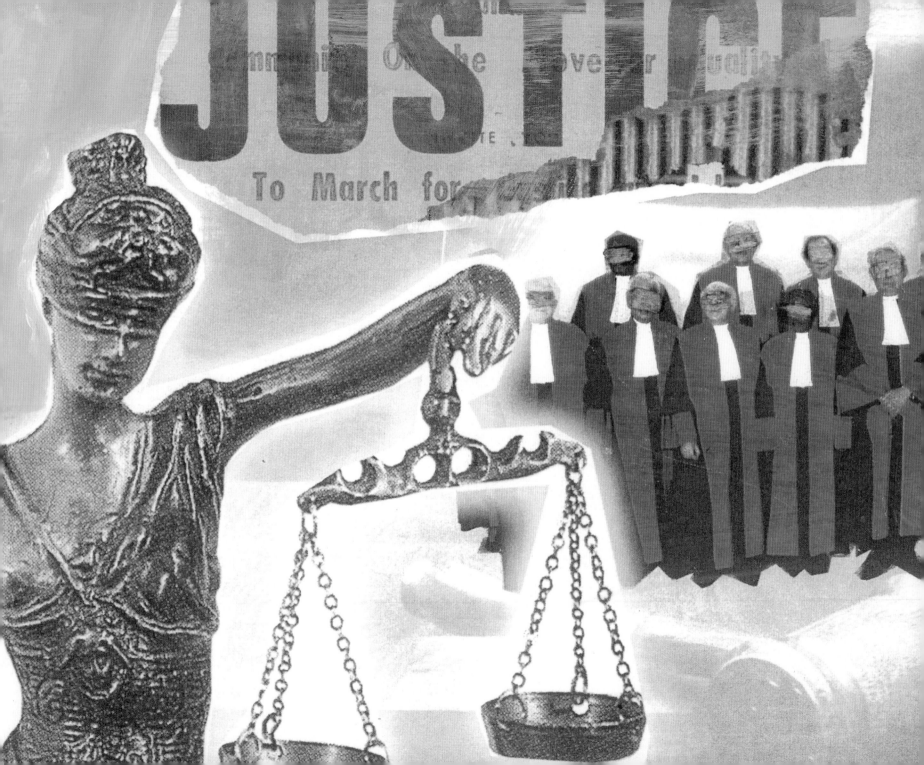

I dream for you
a world

Where community is your home

Where laughter lives with you

And where you're safe and you can roam

I dream for you
a world

Where your home will make you thrive

Providing nourishment and access

A place to bring your dreams alive

I dream for you a world

Where you will share what's
in your mind

Where your actions change
the world

For the good of all mankind

I dream for you a world

Where you'll have knowledge of your past

Old Africa and Southern fields

With abundant dreams so vast

I dream for you a world

Where honest work will
bring you wealth

Where you can plant
financial roots

For your children's future health

turn your dream into a reality.

wealth

I dream for you a world

That values nature and the land

And all the gifts of God's creation

As we respect them with our hands